From a Saint to a King

I would like to dedicate this book to the late George Birtill. It was the information I found in his book *Follow any Stream* that inspired me to write my book about Park Hall. Thank you Mr Birtill (you made a difference).

From a Saint to a King

The History of Park Hall, Charnock Richard

ALEC PRICE

Moorland Publishing

Published by Moorland Publishing
21 Chapel Street, Brinscall, Lancs PR6 8QD

ISBN 0 9549895 0 3

First published 2005

Edited and typeset by
Freelance Publishing Services, Brinscall, Lancs
Printed in Great Britain by
CPL Design and Print, Preston, Lancs.

Acknowledgements

I would like to take this opportunity to thank the following people for the help they gave me with this book.

Firstly a huge thanks to my nephew Stuart Roberts for his wizardry with my computer.

To my friend Joan Appleton for her corrections and guidance.

Similarly to Dr David Sands, for his photographic work and for giving me some valuable advice along the way.

To Mark Harrod, also for his knowledge with computers and digital photography.

To Ray Winstanley and Janet Byers, for their historical knowledge.

To Mr and Mrs Dickinson of Adlington for the use of their wedding photographs.

To the staff at Durham Cathedral, and to Ampleforth Abbey, York.

To Tracy Bruce and her staff at the *Chorley Guardian*.

Thank you to Chorley Library staff, especially the reference library, for their patience.

Tony Flannagan, friend and ex-boss, for photographs and other information.

To John Rigby for giving me his time for interviews and

for photographs.

To Jim Longton. My time spent with Jimmy the Dowser was truly enlightening.

A massive thanks to Mark Leader, Park Hall's Operations Director and his staff for the time, information and photographs both given and loaned to me for use in this book.

Another thanks to David Sands for introducing me to Frances Hackeson. Without her multi-skills this project may have never got off the computer and into book form. Thank you Frances.

Last but certainly not least. To my wife, Brenda … her patience has been tested!

Introduction

The long and diverse history that is Park Hall's own unique story, 'vaguely' became known to me in 1974. I was at that time employed there as the assistant manager of the swimming pool. It wasn't until 2002, however, that I began to learn just how much history Park Hall really had.

All I ever knew about Park Hall during the 1970s was that it had been home to some of Lancashire's most influential families and of course the many ghost stories that always accompany such old historic buildings. It has amazed me that no one has bothered to write Park Hall's story before now. Perhaps everyone (like me) thought it was just another old hall that had been some 'rich Squire's' house for years and was quite boring ... How wrong!

That illusion was shattered one day during a visit to Chorley Library. I was browsing through the local history section when I came across a book by a man called George Birtill. Mr Birtill was a renowned writer and had been the editor of our 'local rag' the *Chorley Guardian*. The book was called *Follow Any Stream*. In his book Mr Birtill had a couple of pages giving a brief account of Park Hall's history. It wasn't much, but it was more than enough to set me thinking.

*Camelot's own King Arthur, looking very regal and in command.
Photograph © Park Hall.*

What made my eyes open was a paragraph that stated,

'Park Hall's story began in the seventh century and had been the resting place for monks who had been travelling for seven years with the Body of St Cuthbert ... in a stone coffin!

I had taken up writing seriously only two years prior to this and I was hungry to learn more about Park Hall and St Cuthbert. I searched my local library and bookshops alike, but there was nothing. However, I was determined to find out more. I then intended to write an article and send it off to *Lancashire Life* magazine. I began my research and interviewed people who had been involved with Park Hall, such as John Rigby. John had been the man who owned and developed Park Hall during the 1970s. I also spoke to Mark Leader, the current Managing Director. Both were very helpful, as were the people at Durham Cathedral, where St Cuthbert's monastic see is based.

After my research was complete I began to write. By the time I had written what I believed to be a fair and honest account, I ended up with something that resembled a short story. I knew it would be far too long for submission to any magazine so I tried to cut it back and tighten it up here and there, yet I still had over 2,000 words. To have cut any more would have been detrimental to the story of what has gone on at Park Hall since its beginning and by now I had my teeth into it in such a way that I was not going to do that. So I have written it in the form of this book.

The decision to write a book meant that I had to do a lot more in-depth research and in doing so I have uncovered some areas of Park Hall's history that are best described as 'grey areas'. However I am going to let you, the reader, make up your own mind. It may be fact or it maybe folklore … But remember! There is no smoke without fire!

View of the lake as it is today. Photograph by Alec Price.

1

St Cuthbert's Life and the Journey After his Death

In the year 634 AD somewhere in the vicinity of Melrose, a Saxon boy was born. This young man was to make such an impact upon so many people's lives, both from his time, right up until the present time.

His name was Cuthbert.

At the age of sixteen Cuthbert was tending sheep on the hills above Melrose when he received a vision of the soul of St Aiden being carried to heaven by angels. It may have been this vision that convinced him to take up holy orders. Although he didn't rush into this calling. Instead he spent some time as a soldier, probably in the service of the Kingdom of Northumbria against the attacks of King Penda of Mercia. After the conflict was ended, Cuthbert entered the monastery at Melrose.

Cuthbert hadn't been there long before he began to make an impression upon Abbot Eata and his other superiors within the monastic community. It was soon apparent that Cuthbert had many special qualities and it was plain to see that this young Monk would go far. He worked hard and his faith in God shone through. With Abbot Eata, Cuthbert moved to Ripon to start a new Monastery. Alcfrith had given an estate for this use but he insisted that the monks adopt Roman customs; not happy with this the Melrose monks retired from Ripon and were succeeded by Wilfred. Cuthbert was made Prior of Melrose in 661.

During this period he spent much of his time undertaking missionary journeys all over the North East. He was well loved by all who knew him, his zeal and his charm endeared him to all and it is said that he had gifts of healing and prophecy. In 663/4 Cuthbert did adopt Roman customs and became Prior of Lindisfarne, where through his patience and persistence he gradually won over the monks; they eventually followed his points of view. A few years later he became a hermit, living on an island adjacent to Lindisfarne – *today, that island is known as St Cuthbert's Isle*. In 676 Cuthbert gave up his office as Prior of Lindisfarne; he withdrew to Inner Farne where he lived in almost complete solitude.

By 685 word had spread through visitors from Lindisfarne and elsewhere of Cuthbert's qualities and his holiness. He had become so famous that King Egfrith and Archbishop Theodore chose him to become the Bishop of Hexham. Almost immediately Cuthbert exchanged this see with Eata for that of Lindisfarne. Sadly however, Cuthbert died at Inner Farne on 20th March 687 following a painful illness and after only two years as Bishop. He was buried at Lindisfarne.

Eleven years later, when his body was being elevated to a shrine in the church, it was discovered that his body was in perfect condition. It was described as 'Incorrupt'.

In 875 Lindisfarne was attacked by Vikings and burned to the ground. Shortly before the Vikings landed, members of Cuthbert's community removed his body and his relics from the shrine and fled. As Lindisfarne burned that night they set off on a journey that was to last for one hundred and twenty years. Travelling with Cuthbert's body on a cart, they first headed for Scotland in the hope they would be able to hide in the hills from Vikings and other grave-robbers. Scotland was a fiercely religious country and the monks knew they would be protected. After travelling across Scotland they headed down into North West England, and it is believed that they went to Whitehaven. Their intention was to take a ship to Ireland, but for some reason they didn't, but instead they made their way to Carlisle. The Melrose monks were known to have had connections at Carlisle. There they knew they would be sure of some support and supplies before moving on.

The story is that St Cuthbert's body was brought to Lancashire and hidden for three years in woodland where Park Hall now stands. Local historian George Birtill wrote :

'St Cuthbert's body was brought to Park Hall after a seven year journey in a stone coffin.'

Quite how this story came about is not known. I can find no written proof that this ever happened. Lancashire didn't exist until after the Normans arrived in 1066. This part of the world, from the River Ribble down to the River Mersey was known as South Western Northumbria and was only inhabited by around two to three thousand people, of which probably few could write anyway. So if St Cuthbert was brought here, it would only have become knowledge by word of mouth. Regarding the tale that he was transported in a 'stone coffin', Durham Cathedral have reliably informed me that he was moved around in a wooden coffin.

If St Cuthbert was brought to these parts after seven years of travelling, then it would have been in the year 882 that he arrived at Park Hall, and if indeed he was hidden in the woods for three years, he would have been moved on in 885/6. I say if, because there is no concrete proof that his body was ever brought there.

After the monks moved on, it is believed that in 908 a monastery was built of stone upon the site. Again, there is no written proof of this. Excavations that took place in the 1970s unearthed foundations which some people believed were parts of that monastery. Park Hall ground was rich in red sandstone. Many of the buildings that stand on the site today include some of that stone and it is clearly visible in the walls. George Birtill claimed that the 908 monastery was built by Benedictine monks. Again, however, there is considerable doubt to his theory. Both the Benedictine orders at Ampleforth Abbey and Durham Cathedral believe that there were very few Benedictine monks in this country until after the arrival of the Normans in 1066. Mind you, that's not to say that Benedictine monks didn't come to Park Hall after 1066. If they did, then that may well have led to the theory that it was they who built the monastery, especially if they were still around when Sir Henry De Lea arrived on the scene.

Because of the timing of the monastery, it is more than likely that monks from St Cuthbert's own community stayed after the others left. It is thought they built the monastery to commemorate St Cuthbert having been there.

Despairing of the fact that there are so many grey areas attached to these early years, I have gone to some very unusual lengths to try to find the truth. One avenue I explored was to enrol the help of Mr Jim Longton. Mr Longton is a 'dowser'. When you mention 'dowsing' most people conjure up in their minds someone walking around with two sticks, trying to find water underground. I can assure you, there is much more to dowsing than that. Jimmy Longton, who is 74, and is from Euxton, is renowned the world over for his skills. Indeed he is held in such high regard by fellow dowsers that he has been dubbed the best in Britain. Some years ago he was paid £45,000 by the Treasury after finding a large cache of Viking silver near Carlisle. More recently he has located the wreck of King Charles's royal baggage ferry, which sank in the Firth of Forth in 1633, containing a priceless cargo of silver, gifts and jewels. Experts had been searching for the ship for years, until an American company heard of Jimmy and enlisted his help. Jim first dowsed an Admiralty map of the area and then went to the Firth of Forth and pinpointed the exact same site one mile offshore. Sonar confirmed the find.

I had heard of Jimmy Longton from my daughter years before as he used to amaze her with his tales when he called into her insurance office in Chorley. I was reminded of him more recently because of a TV show he had done with Jane Goldman, the wife of presenter Jonathan Ross. I rang Jimmy and told him about Park Hall and my dilemma over St Cuthbert and also the monastery. He immediately agreed to help; in fact he told me there and then to 'Come round to my house and pick me up, we'll go up there now' – and we did! I have to admit I felt a bit conspicuous following Jim around Park Hall's grounds, with him holding his dowsing rod out in front of him and talking out loud to it! It was quite a nice day and there were a lot of people about so we got some very enquiring looks! Not least from Park Hall's Managing Director, Mark Leader – I half expected him to call for the men in white coats!   However, soon Jim was coming up with answers to my questions. He pinpointed an underground tunnel that he told me was about twenty feet down but that it had either caved in or been filled in. This made sense, and more about that later. On the question of a monastery, Jim mapped out – with the help of his rod – the outline of what he described as a church or chapel. It was only small, but the amazing thing was it was only a few feet from where the 908AD foundations were located in the 1970s. Jimmy Longton's dowsing skills confirmed that some of the stone used in the older buildings was from pre-Norman times. He also told me that there were six ghosts in residence in various parts of Park Hall. Again, more about that later. Jimmy Longton is a wonderful character and his talents are not to be scoffed at. Dowsing is a centuries-old skill and it works!

It is also possible that once the monks had arrived at Park Hall, St Cuthbert's body was laid to rest in a coffin carved out of 'stone'. Much of the stone used was dug from three quarries, or 'delphs' on the site, by the monks, the last remaining quarry being where the lake is now at the front of the hotel.

After the monks moved on from Park Hall they are known to have rested at Northampton-on-Tweed, Ripon and Chester-le-street, where King Athelstan offered 96lbs silver, two gospel books and a book of his life to the shrine. It may be just a coincidence, but King Athelstan was also the ruler of south western Northumbria (Lancashire) at this time.

St Cuthbert's body was at Chester-le-street for many years until a second threatened invasion by the Scandinavians prompted the monks to move to Ripon. After a time his body was moved back to Chester-le-street. It was when they took the decision to move again from Chester-le-street that a strange thing happened. The cart with St Cuthbert's body on it became very heavy and would not move. One of the monks said he had had a vision and had been told that they should go to Durham. When the decision was finally taken to go to Durham, the cart moved easily and freely. The monks reached their final destination, Durham, in 995.

St Cuthbert's body was laid to rest and a Saxon church was built over the shrine.

St Cuthbert's relics were placed into the shrine in 999. In 1104, St Cuthbert and his relics were transferred to a new Norman Cathedral. Once again his body was examined and pronounced incorrupt. This was witnessed by observers who were originally sceptical.

The saint's remains were last examined in 1828. His bones were reburied but his secondary relics are now housed in the monastic buildings at Durham.

As to whether or not he was ever at Park Hall, we might never know, but Durham Cathedral have not discounted the possibility. I personally believe it to be true – a wonderfully romantic story like this has to be true! It is also a fact that a monastery, or some kind of religious centre, was built there in 908. Whatever you make of this tale, you must take into account, as I have said before … 'There's no smoke without fire!'

I often try to imagine what it must have been like for those monks: the hardships they must have endured as they began their journey. A journey that was to last for one hundred and twenty years before St Cuthbert was finally laid to rest at Durham. Maybe it was something like this …

Looking out to sea a young boy spotted Viking longboats: fifty or more were approaching. Luckily the wind that usually blew in so strongly off the Northumbrian coast had abated and the Vikings were having to row the last few miles to shore. The young Saxon boy ran to the town and raised the alarm. This gave the members of the Lindisfarne community a chance to prepare and gather their possessions before fleeing. This was especially worrying for members of the monastic order in Lindisfarne. They knew that the Vikings would rob and plunder their church and probably desecrate the tomb and shrine of St Cuthbert.

No time was to be lost: they had to remove St Cuthbert from his grave, pack up his relics and the shrine. Quickly, with the help of the townsfolk, they did what they had to do and loaded St Cuthbert's coffin onto one cart and the other possessions onto more carts. They knew they would be slow to make their escape. There wasn't enough time to get far before the invaders would catch up with them, so a plan was hurriedly put into action. It was decided that members of the townsfolk would go off in one direction, making as much noise as possible and creating a diversion. While this was going on, the monks with St Cuthbert's body and his shrine would head north-west, where they would hide in woodland just three miles from Lindisfarne. They were to remain there until darkness fell and then move off. They knew that after nightfall the Vikings would not follow them.

As the monks looked down through the darkness towards Lindisfarne, they could see the whole town was on fire and with great sadness they set off, heading towards the Scottish border. There were some thirty of them in number. Some were no more than boys in their teens and some were old men. One thing none of them knew when they set off, is how long they would be gone, and I doubt if any of them could have imagined that their wanderings would not end until one hundred and twenty years had passed. Indeed the only person to complete the journey from beginning to end was St Cuthbert himself.

It was seven years later that they arrived at the River Ribble, where they would have found a settlement of monks. These were more than likely to have been Celtic monks. The settlement was known as 'Priestown' but today it's called Preston. As they moved further south about ten miles into what is now the heart of Lancashire they found much of the terrain to be harsh and inhospitable. However the land around Park Hall was very fertile and densely wooded. The marshlands to the west would provide fish and the moors and woods were full of animals. It was a place where they felt safe and could be self-sufficient. They built a small settlement in the woods and remained there for three years.

This place was to become Park Hall .... But not for another three hundred years!

The time between the monks being at Park Hall and the arrival of the Normans is again another grey area. No one knows whether the monks were still in residence or not. Three hundred years is a long time. It is possible that the original monastic order could have faded out and sometime after 1066 the Benedictine monks – knowing of the St Cuthbert connection – moved in. This would give credence to early theories that the first buildings were put there by Benedictines. However, unless the site is excavated properly by archaeologists, we will probably never really know the truth.

2

The Normans

The arrival of the Norman Lords brought some degree of organisation to south-west Northumbria. In 1086 the lands between the Ribble and the Mersey were given to Roger of Poitou, who was the son of Earl Roger of Montgomery. This gift was his reward for his part in the Conquest. As a reward to his men at arms he gave the land that we now know as Park Hall to a William Banastre who in turn gave it to Sir Henry de Lea in return for a favour. On this estate Sir Henry de Lea built his manor house. He described it as 'The hall in the beautiful parkland', hence it became known as 'Park Hall'.

Sir Henry held the moiety (a half share) of the lands around Park Hall with Richard de Charnock. Subsequently the area became known as Charnock Richard. Sir Henry de Lea continued to take stone from the quarries to build his estate. Although the de Charnocks were the family who gave their name to the district, they were never the owners, nor did they live at, Park Hall. They were, however, very strong Catholic adherents, as were the de Lea's and the de Hoghton's, who lived at Park Hall later on. Through their religion they had very close connections and supported each other in many ways.

Two hundred years later Sir Henry de Lea (another Sir Henry, I suspect?) was granted a Royal Charter by Edward I to hold a market each Friday on his manor of Charnock. He was also granted 'free warren' to hunt and fish etc, providing he didn't do so on land which belonged to the royal forests, nor must he allow outlaws to seek refuge anywhere on his lands. The latter was a condition he was to break on a massive scale some years later.

Thirty years on from this, in 1315, Lancashire had grown considerably. No longer was it just the lands between the Ribble and the Mersey. Lancashire stretched many miles into the Lake District. Lancaster was now the local capital and Earl Thomas of Lancaster ruled the roost. Every small district had its local knight or baron. Robert de Holland was one such baron. He was made chief domestic official by the Earl of Lancaster. On receiving this office he was given lands in Cheshire and Staffordshire. These awards of such wealth stirred jealousy amongst other noblemen. None more so than Adam Banastre and although Holland and Banastre had once been united in an earlier dispute, this raked up an old feud that dated back as far as 1268 to a time when a Holland had spoiled his fishponds and had taken off with his wife and daughter for a day. The showering of these gifts raised Banastre's anger so much that in 1315 he raised a rebellion against Holland and Thomas Earl of Lancaster. It became known as the 'Banastre Rebellion'. Adam Banastre led his supporters to Wingates on 8th October and there three other knights joined him. They were Sir Henry de Lea of Charnock Richard, Sir Thomas Banastre (Brother of Adam) and Sir William Bradshaigh of Haigh, Wigan.

Translation of the market charter granted to Sir Henry de Lea of Park Hall by King Edward I

And to the Archbishops etc., Greeting.

Know that we have granted and by this charter have confirmed unto our dear and faithful Henry de Lea that he and his heirs may in perpetuity hold a market each week on Friday on his manor Charnok in the county of Lancaster, also a fair of three days duration that is the eve, the feast and the morrow of St Nicholas provided that the market and the fair are not detrimental to the neighbouring markets and fairs. We also grant to the same Henry and his heirs in perpetuity free warren on all his demesne lands of Lee, Charnok, Ravensmoeles and quelton-on-Dunnolmesmores, in the county aforesaid, provided that those lands are not within the limits of our forest and further that no man enter those lands as a fugitive or to take anything which may belong the warren without licence and wish of Henry himself or of his heirs upon paid of or forfeit of £10. Wherefore it is our wish etc., that the aforesaid manor with all its liberties and free customs touching a market and fairs of such a kind providing the market and the fair are not detrimental to the neighbouring markets and fairs.

The following being witnesses:

The Venerable R. Bishop of Bath and Wells, Our Chancellor, Richard de Burgh, Earl of Ulster Reginald de Grey, Thomas de Clare, Richard de Brus, John de Monte Alto, Eustace of Hache and others.

Given under our hand at Chester 15th day of September (1284).

That day the four of them took an oath to live and die together, after which they set about raising an army. By the time they had finished they had gathered some 800 men and on 22nd October they marched to Charnock Richard where they were joined by members of the Mawdsley family, and men from Preston, Chorley, Coppull, Charnock Richard and Haigh. The army of rebels marched against all the large towns in south Lancashire including Liverpool and Manchester, where they raided the home of Sir Henry de Trafford and took a banner from the church bearing the king's arms, after which they told people they had received it from the monarch, using it as a sign that they had the king's approval for their activities. Moving on, they plundered as much wealth as they could along the way, in order to fund their rebellion. By doing this they made quite a few enemies. They sent men to Clitheroe Castle for arms (they were stored there for use against invading Scots).

On 4th November the rebel army reached Preston. Earl Neville, in command of the Duke of Lancaster's forces (about 600 men), divided his army into two companies. He sent one company against the rebels and kept one in reserve. His first attack was defeated on the outskirts of Preston, after which the rebels entered Preston and looted the town. Later that same day Thomas Earl of Lancaster and Robert de Holland ordered the reserve army to attack. After an hour's fighting Sir William Bradshaigh and his men fled the field (and later the country). This heralded the end of the rebellion. Thomas Banastre was captured and placed in gaol at Lancaster. Adam Banastre and Henry de Lea escaped and hid for eight days on Leyland Moor and in woods. Two days later Sir Robert de Holland along with 2,000 men entered Leyland hundred. Eventually Banastre and De Lea were found hiding at the house of Henry de Furlong, who it is said, had betrayed them. Surrounded by 300 men they were soon taken and without trial were beheaded there and then on Leyland Moor.

Meanwhile, back at Park Hall all this left Sir Henry's son William as Lord of the manor. In 1320 William's daughter, Sibilla de Lea (a direct descendant of Lady Godiva, on her mother's side) married Sir Richard de Hoghton, of Hoghton Tower. This was the beginning of a new dynasty at Park Hall, one that was to last for almost 400 years in one way and another. The De Hoghtons* were very often torn between obeying and disobeying the crown. Their loyalties depended largely upon religion. Being very strong Catholics, they often put their faith in God before their allegiance to the crown. Things did calm down for many years and at times the de Hoghton's were known to have rented out Park Hall.

They were back in trouble again around 1575. Thomas Hoghton had left the country to go to Antwerp without obtaining a Queen's licence. (*The Queen's licence was the forerunner of today's passport*). On 16th March Queen Elizabeth granted a licence to Richard Hoghton of Park Hall, for him to go to Antwerp to persuade Thomas to return under a bond of £200 and within two months. It is believed that Richard was the illegitimate son of Thomas's father. (It was a recognised thing for the illegitimate children of Lords and Earls etc. to be housed in the same manor and to sometimes take the father's name, especially if the mother was of 'high birth'. Whilst this

---

* De Hoghtons and Hoghtons are the same family. They all originate from the De Hoghtons of Hoghton Tower. The Park Hall Hoghtons dropped the 'De' for some reason. But I'm not sure at what point or why. The De Leas were always De Leas.

was accepted, it was legitimate children who inherited first, in order of birth. The illegitimate children were often named too, as 'base' brothers or sisters to the legitimate children.) Richard was unsuccessful in talking his brother into returning. Thomas died in Liege and was buried at Douay in 1580.

A letter written by Thomas Hoghton in Antwerp to his half brother Richard Hoghton of Park Hall, Charnock Richard. Dated 6th May 1576.

Trusty and well beloved

These maybe to signify unto you that I am in good health. I sent you a letter by Richard Bardsley. I know not whether you have received ytt or no. wherefore I wold dysyre you to helpe me with a sett of recorders of ye best sort and to send them to me by one or pagemen which the post or other wyse as you can. The other letter yath I wrote to you afore was to dysyre you to come over att wytson-tyde yf you could get your lycence of Earl of ye Casell and your bysness well despatched. Oft time I dysyre you to come over yf you can gett lycence or els not. I ssent you in my letter of ye overthrow of ye Kings enemies which was a great overthrow there is come to Antwerp three thousand Spannerth [Spaniards] which mayd three peels of shootiinge of there gunns ye like hath not bine herd in Antwerp and put ye towne in great feyre of being sacked ye Speannerth we are behinde of there wages two and twenty months and for ye overthrow which they gave the Kings enemies ther request was that ye might have ther wages of ye towne or else they wold spoyle ye towne the townsmen perceiving that was sor afreyed in so much they pay to ye govenor off ye confere to ye Kings men and to ye sogers [soldiers] two hundred thousand all upon one day which I think is a very great some to be payed within one cittye. I wold dysyre you to send me worde by your letter as soon as ye can whether ye can come yourself. I dysyre you to speke to ? To come to me afore lady day thus refraining to trouble you any further at this tiyme from Antwerp this 6th day of May.

Your assured brother

Thomas Hoghton.

Postscript, ytt is reported that Lodewefse ye Prince of Orange brother is dede in a towne ye district of Cliveland called wish we louke for ye Kings fleet every day ye which I trust will behier in has yff God send a feyre wynd and then I trust this cptery will grow in quietness. The Prince of Orange hath requested of yet towns in Holland there to give xx tonnes of gold to mayntain his sogers against ye Kings fleet or else to give two tonnes of giold and to go from them.

Much of the illegitimacy of these times could be blamed on the diet of the day. The Elizabethans ate so much meat it is said this is what led to them being so virile! Food prices started a fairly steep climb and by 1572 The court of the Lord Mayor and Aldermen fixed them. From 4th April 1572 the prices were as follows.

| Best Swan | 6s 8d |
| Cygnet | 6s 0d |

Stork	4s 0d
Pelican	2s 0d
Goose	1s 2d
Best Gree Geese until May day 9d.	
Best Chickens	4d.
Larks	8d per dozen.
Blackbirds	1s per dozen.
Butter	3d per lb until All Hallows

Best eggs 4 for a penny or 1 farthing each until Ash Wednesday.

Despite rising prices, artisans lived well. Most people ate three meals a day beginning with breakfast at about 6 a.m. (daybreak) This would consist of bread, salt herring, cold meat pottage, cheese and ale.

At midday in towns they ate in taverns or bought food at a cook shop, such as hot sheep's feet, mackerel soup, oysters, ribs of beef. Rancid meat pies were also provided together with bread and ale and fruit in season.

On ordinary days the well-to-do made do with a piece of beef or a loin of veal, 2 chickens and oranges for dinner.

Supper might be a shoulder of mutton, two rabbits, pigs 'pettie toes', cold beef and cheese.

With all this protein, it is little wonder they had so much vitality.

It was around this same time that the Jesuit Edmund Campion was being outlawed for his refusal to return to the Church of England. Edmund Campion had originally been a deacon in the Church of England in 1569, but, troubled by his conscience, he went on a pilgrimage to Rome and later joined the Catholic church. History states that for a time in the year 1581 he stayed at Park Hall where he published Catholic propaganda. He was arrested later that year. He was to be allowed to live, on condition he returned to the Church of England. He refused and was charged with conspiracy against the Crown. He was sentenced to death, put on the rack and executed. On the rack he was forced to disclose the names of those who had given him shelter – among those he mentioned was Richard Hoghton of Park Hall. Because of this the Queen's Commissioners were told to keep a close eye on Park Hall.

Richard Hoghton died in 1622 leaving two children: Anne, who was married to Thomas Bradley, and William Hoghton. Park Hall was left to Richard's younger child William, who had a daughter also named Anne, who was said to be a lunatic, and her allowance was stopped. William Hoghton was said to have been at the burning of Lancaster. During the Civil War William fought on the king's side and he was made a Lieutenant Colonel. He was killed in the first battle of Newbury in 1643. As a result, Parliament wasted no time in confiscating the estate. Park Hall was re-sold ten years later and the purchasers, who were Hugh Diconson and Robert Holt, were believed to have bought it on behalf of John Hoghton, who in any case recorded the pedigree of his son William there.

Again the Hoghton family adhered to the Catholic faith. They were known to have given shelter to many a priest, including a Father Barlow, who was a much travelled priest. He is said to have done most of his ministering in the dead of night and was almost caught on several occasions. William Hoghton is believed to have saved his life after he had been shot by Protestant supporters while out one night. This story is included in the book *Moon in Scorpio* by Robert Neill.

In 1683 William Hoghton married Elizabeth Dalton of Thurnham, Lancaster. The Hoghton name was resident at

Park Hall up until 1710, when after the death of Elizabeth's father, she consequently became heiress to the family estate at Thurnham. With this they changed their name to Dalton and moved to the much larger estate at Thurnham, renting off Park Hall. It is not known how long Park Hall was rented out for, but the Hoghtons were back in residence by the time of the Jacobite rebellion in 1715. Or at least, one William Hoghton was back there at that time, along with John Dalton and others who leased off various parts of the estate.

A view of the square. This shows the old of the Banqueting Hall with that of the new hotel. Photograph by Dr David Sands.

3

The Jacobite Rebellion

The Jacobite uprising in 1715 again brought problems for everyone who had anything to do with Park Hall. Because the Hoghtons and the Daltons both supported the Stuart cause, and with the Jacobites being defeated at Preston, this heralded disaster for all concerned. Estates were again confiscated and tenants were evicted if it was proved they sided with the Jacobites. A letter from William Hoghton to the Rev. James Woods of Chowbent, read:

The officers here desire to march at break of day to Preston, they desire me to raise what men I can to meet us at Preston tomorrow. So desire you to raise all the force you can – I mean lusty young fellows to draw up on Cuerden Green, to be by Ten o'clock. To bring with them what arms they have fit for service and scythes put in straight poles and such as have not, to bring spades and bill hooks for pioneering with. Pray go immediately all amongst your neighbours and give this notice.

I am your faithful servant

W. Hoghton

The Jacobite army 'Supporters of James II' had marched from Scotland to Derby on their way to London. After turning back at Derby they were quartered in the Chorley area overnight, perhaps even at Park Hall.

John Dalton, who had been in gaol at Lancaster Castle until the Jacobites released him, was known to have rented part of Park Hall in 1721.

In 1751 on 26th August Edward Hoghton O.S.B., former chaplain at Park Hall, was executed along with his brother Robert Hoghton, charged with high treason.

After this Park Hall was again home to a number of tenants. This was the way until the estate was sold in 1789 to Mr

A photograph of Park Hall taken in 1903. Henry Alison was the owner at this time. A well-respected gentleman, he was the Lancashire County Treasurer. In my opinion, Park Hall has never looked so resplendent. Photograph © Park Hall

William German after which it passed down the female side of the family and eventually descended to his great-grandson Henry Alison. Mr German had been a mining entrepreneur. Park Hall at that time boasted a mine that produced the finest quality coal. Of all the mines around, the Park Hall seam was said to have been of the best quality.

When Henry Alison lived at Park Hall he was a very well respected man and somewhat eccentric – for all his wealth he insisted on walking to and from home to Euxton station every day on his way to work. He was the Lancashire County Treasurer. Very often he would be accompanied on his walk by people who wished to discuss their business with him.

In the 1851 census Richard Alison was named as head of the household, he was the son of Alice Alison. In 1861 Richard's wife, also called Alice Alison, was named as head of the household. Henry Alison was the son of the first Alice, who died in 1839 leaving five sons and five daughters. Henry died at Park Hall in 1915.

After this, much of Park Hall was sold off and little is known about the people who lived there, except that a Mr Joseph Smith lived there in 1925. It is believed he bought the Hall in 1919. Later on a Mr Ibzan Sagar was the owner, though what he did during his time at Park Hall is unclear.

Banqueting Hall from across the square. Photograph by Alec Price.

4

The Three Fives Club

The year 1933 saw the arrival of George Victor Few and the good times were at last about to come to Park Hall. The past 800 years had seen Park Hall have many a conflict and many family feuds. Now with the twentieth century well established, and the First World War behind them, the Fews had taken over at Park Hall and a feeling of excitement and anticipation was in the air. Although there was the Depression of the 1930s to contend with, and Mr Hitler was also waiting in the wings to upset things, George Victor Few had high hopes for his beautiful Park Hall and he began to put his plans into action.

In 1942 Park Hall was a Gentleman's club; it was a very exclusive establishment and was only open to members. It was not easy to obtain membership – more a case of who you knew. Known as 'The Three Fives Club', many of the members were well-to-do businessmen or people of high standing in the community. Certainly the only ladies allowed in were by special invitation. Word had it that occasionally ladies of ill repute were known to have been invited, for what reason, we can only guess! Much of what went on in the early days of The Three Fives Club is only speculation. This is because it

The Dining Room — with Fully Licensed Restaurant

The Hall, built about the year 908 A.D. by the Benedictine Monks, was to commemorate the resting places of St. Cuthbert in 643 A.D., during his seven years journey in his stone coffin as a protection against body snatchers. This historical building has bravely withstood the vicissitudes and storms of a tempestuous past. Successive owners down to the present time have added new features to keep the place in step with modern requirements. It is a tribute to their reverence for the grandeur and nobility of a bygone age that these new features never obtrude themselves on the eye, never jar on that old, solid dignity which shews that they had a deep-rooted pride and admiration for this century-scarred heritage — the work of craftsmen who built for more than many tomorrows.

Today, Park Hall Hotel can accommodate in the Dining Room up to 60 guests and 300 in the large Restaurant. It is ideal for private parties and weddings.

Good food and service in the atmosphere of a secluded country guest house are under the careful supervision of the genial hosts ...

Mr. and Mrs. George Victor Few

(Top) Drawing of the Dining Room when George Few was at Park Hall. This drawing accompanied the advertisement (bottom). Both illustrations provided by Park Hall.

was such a closed shop, so the tales that did get through were indeed the gossip of the day. It is also said that members indulged in 'Dog fighting and Cock fighting', there was some evidence of this when later redevelopment at Park Hall uncovered what were believed to be 'baiting pits'.

In general, though, Park Hall under George Few's ownership was a well respected and well run country house. He also used the hall as a 'Boxers retreat'. Well-known boxers would come and stay at Park Hall prior to a big fight. George Few had a part of the Hall set up for them to train in. When John Rigby took over he found photographs of some of the boxers who had stayed there.

Mr Few did a lot for the people of the surrounding areas and he opened his grounds for summer garden parties. One

Mr and Mrs Dickinson's wedding party, taken in front of Park Hall Hotel. Kevin and Joan Dickinson held their wedding reception at Park Hall in 1960. Some 70 guests were in attendance and George Few and his wife were hosts. Photograph provided by Mr and Mrs Dickinson.

Mr and Mrs Dickinson's wedding day – at the lakeside. Photograph provided by Mr and Mrs Dickinson.

Saturday afternoon the residents of Chorley, Coppull and Charnock Richard were surprised when a stagecoach from the Royal Umpire museum at Croston passed through the streets. On board and in period costume were many members of The Three Fives club. In charge of the team of horses was Mr J. B. Kevill, of Gradwell's Farm, Croston. Also on board were Councillor R. Morris, J.P., chairman of Chorley Rural District Council and the Deputy Mayor of Chorley, Councillor A. R. Sheppard, J.P. This was to set the scene for 'Ye olde ancient fayre of St Botulph's Day'. They then jointly opened the fayre in the secluded grounds of Park Hall. A large attendance enjoyed music by St Georges Pipe Band and there were dancing displays by the Mar-Jan School of Dancing.

In the evening the music was by the Black and White Five Minstrels and the Three Fives Band. Visitors enjoyed tours of the hall, where there were suits of armour dating back to the twelfth and fourteenth centuries on view, which would have been reminiscent of centuries of past warfare. Inside the Hall many examples of craftsman's art would have been admired in the wood panelling and the old beams.

In later years George Few and his wife opened Park Hall for other things. It could be said that George Few was the first to open it as a 'leisure centre'. He advertised it as having been 'Built for service 908 A.D. – Still giving the best service'.

Benedictine monks originally built Park Hall about the year 908 A.D.

Sketch depicting monks building Park Hall's monastery in 908 AD. Drawing provided by Park Hall.

ᴘᴀʀᴋ Hᴀʟʟ — CHARNOCK RICHARD, STEEPED IN HISTORY AND SONG, INVITES YOU TO ACCEPT IT'S HOSPITALITY AND PLEASURES INDOORS AND OUT.

ᴘᴀʀᴋ Hᴀʟʟ is situated two miles to the west of Chorley adjacent to the M6 Motorway at Charnock Richard. It lies in secluded woodland aloof from the fret, fume and flutter of the outer world; yet it is only the sweep of its beautiful drive removed from the highway of life.

Coming up the inveigling drive, the vista across the lake to where it loses itself in the distance is enchanting. A silver birch, like a sentinel in the wood, gives an alluring gladness to the mind that is not easily forgotten. This beautiful view has all the warmth of a lover's kiss. The lake, spreading itself out before the Hall, is surrounded by benignant trees of many varieties ... streaked by that lovely lady, the silver birch, while the masses of rhododendron in full bloom make an arresting picture.

Another of George Few's advertisements. Probably a later one as it mentions the M6 motorway, but just as beautifully worded. Provided by Park Hall.

It became known as 'Park Hall Hotel and Country Club. 200 acres, 50 acres of woodland, 5 acres of lakes, available for walks – fishing – shooting'. The Hall was used for weddings and many other kinds of functions. Complete day outings could be booked for 25s all-inclusive.

Some of George Few's advertisements were written with such eloquent dialogue that I could imagine them having been written by Leonard Sachs, the presenter of the old time music hall TV show 'The Good Old Days'. His description of the Hall and grounds was first class.

George Victor Few was the owner of Park Hall for almost forty years. Sadly, in that time it would appear that he hardly

A sketch of the Lounge Bar. Drawing provided by Park Hall.

ever spent any money on improving the Hall, or on any kind of restoration work. This naturally meant deterioration set in and in some areas of the building it was disastrous. Much of the crafted woodwork became infested with woodworm and dry rot was also rife. By 1970 George Few was an old man, in poor health and no longer able to carry on running such a huge place. The Hall was in a bad state of disrepair and the grounds were overgrown and he had no choice but to sell Park Hall.

(Opposite) One of George Few's eloquently worded advertisements for Park Hall. Provided by Park Hall. (Below) Aerial view of Park Hall taken around the time of the sale by George Few to John Rigby in 1972. The whole site was by then looking very run down. Photograph © Park Hall.

Front view of the hotel entrance as it is today. Photograph by Alec Price.

5

Park Hall's Re-birth

As George Few was preparing to put Park Hall on the market, a young man was emerging on the scene who was at that time, without doubt, one of the North West's most prolific property developers. His name was John Rigby. Although John had mostly involved himself in the housing market, he had recently just opened his first restaurant, the Cuerden Manor. He was also involved with – through his building business – a man called Trevor Hemmings. Mr Hemmings is now one of the richest men in the country and owns a lot of property in Blackpool, including Blackpool Tower. Trevor Hemmings had heard through the grapevine of George Few's intention to sell Park Hall and suggested to John that it might be just the place for his next restaurant venture. John rang George Few and a meeting was arranged.

John Rigby was at the time only 27 years old, but he was already a well-established businessman and a wealthy one. As John reached Park Hall's driveway all he could see was a narrow path through a tunnel of rhododendron bushes. His first thought was for his beautiful new Rolls Royce: would it pass through unscathed? John decided to risk it. As he emerged, he was greeted with the view of the lake to his right and this magnificent old house on the left. John waited for a few moments, taking time to look around. He knew this was the place for him: he could see the massive potential that Park Hall had.

On meeting Mr Few, John pondered that the age difference might go against him but he was soon put at his ease. John found Mr Few to be a wonderful old man and they got on very well. Mr Few showed John all around the buildings. One thing that John Rigby will never forget is the smell of cats. George Few had at least 70 cats around the place – many of them were wild and had never been domesticated (or housetrained) and the place stank!. However this did nothing to put John Rigby off wanting to be the next owner of Park Hall.

John spent seven hours with George Few that day and after quite a bit of tea and a lot of discussion over the purchase price, they parted the best of friends. George Few was asking more than John wanted to, or was prepared to, pay. Eventually John Rigby bought Park Hall for £210,000 – an amazing price when you consider today's house prices!

In 1971 the redevelopment started. The first thing was to remove the cats, which was to prove a monumental task, because they were so wild and even living in the roof of the building, and it was recommended that some of them needed to be shot. Once the cats were out of the way John Rigby began to assemble a vast team of over one hundred builders, joiners and other workers. It was important to get some part of the building open for business as soon as possible. In August 1971 Park Hall was back in business; the first part to be completed was the Banqueting Suite. John had made this his priority because George Few had wedding bookings and John didn't want to let anyone down.

It was soon to become apparent to John that Park Hall was steeped in history and the more John Rigby learnt of its background, the more he delved into it. One day when a builder was knocking a wall down in part of the old Hall, he literally fell through the wall and into a passageway. This turned out to be a priest hole dating back to Elizabethan times. The Hoghtons, who were strong Catholics, used to hide priests and monks from persecution. The passage led down into an underground tunnel that had caved in some years earlier. The tunnel appeared to head down into what is known as 'Kiln Wood', which is where Camelot theme park is now situated. John Rigby dug down some 17ft all around the hotel in an attempt to find more of the tunnel, but with no success. Rumour has it that a main tunnel was once believed to have gone as far as Charnock Richard parish church.

What was found was evidence of some very old foundations. John Rigby called in Burton Barnes, an archaeologist from Preston, who determined that part of the foundation was from around Elizabethan times. He told John the lower part was from earlier than that, possibly as far back as the eleventh century.

Amongst other items found were four enormous stone troughs, or baths as John described them to me. These had been hewn out of some of Park Hall's famous sandstone, believed to have been carved by the monks centuries earlier. These were found buried in years of muck and cow dung. For a time they stood in the square in front of the Banqueting Hall. Two of them are still on site. One is in the Spanish Village complex and one at Camelot.

One of the original four stone troughs or monk's baths as John Rigby described them, now being used as a planter in the Spanish Village complex. This trough was dug up during the redevelopment of 1972. It had been buried for many years under tons of earth. Another can be seen at Camelot theme park. Photograph by Alec Price.

The lake was also drained, the intention being to clean it and make it safe for use as a boating lake. With the water out, more treasures from times past were found. These were in the form of large bottles 2ft long with round bottoms. A lot of what was found at that time was given to museums by John Rigby.

John Rigby on the day he opened Park Hall's Cabaret Lounge, 14th August 1973, his 30th birthday: a very proud young man. Photograph provided by John Rigby.

Entrance to Banqueting Hall including the crest over the door. Photograph by Dr David Sands.

It was because of what John Rigby had told me and the uncertainty of what was supposed to have happened with regard to St Cuthbert and the monastery, that I decided to ring Jimmy Longton (the dowser). My day with Jim was brilliant. As soon as we arrived he asked me what I wanted to know. We walked round to the front of the old part of the hotel and I asked Jim if he could detect anything to do with the tunnel that John Rigby had found. He got to work with his rod: I had never seen this done before and I felt very conspicuous walking with him as he moved around asking his rod to point to the direction of any tunnels. After watching his brass dowsing rod move, first one way and then the other,

Inside the Banqueting Hall. This Hall is said to be built on top of the foundations of the monastery. It has also been the scene of some strange occurrences. Photography by Dr David Sands.

he said 'There's possibly two tunnels'. By this time we had moved around to the side of the hotel, about thirty yards from the entrance to the new hotel complex. Jimmy was still talking to his trusty rod and I was still following like a lap dog, very conscious of everyone watching us. He stopped and asked his rod to point in the direction the tunnel went. It immediately moved and pointed in the direction of Camelot theme park. Camelot had been built in a valley, shown on some maps as 'Kiln wood'. Centuries ago this area would have been very heavily wooded.

From here we walked around to the square, where I asked Jimmy if he could find any evidence of a monastery. At first he asked his rod about the monastery, but got no response.

Jim Longton pictured at the front of the Hall. It was here, he told me, two tunnels had run in two different directions, one towards Charnock Richard parish church and one towards Kiln Wood. Photograph by Alec Price.

Then he re-phrased his question. 'Was there ever a church or chapel here?' His rod moved and pointed towards the Medieval Banqueting Hall. He then began to map out the said building. He dropped his mobile phone on the floor and instructed me to pick it up for him when he'd finished. Moving off again, all the time talking to his rod, he walked toward the side of the building; as soon as the rod moved he stopped and broke off a leaf from a plant, placing it on the floor. This exercise carried on until Jimmy had marked out a square some twenty or so feet in dimension. By now we had a fair sized audience, including one Park Hall employee who could contain his curiosity no longer. When I explained what it was all about, he went away quite intrigued, but happy. The building that Jimmy had marked out was only about ten feet from where John Rigby had found the original foundations although Jimmy Longton had no knowledge of this.

I have no idea how it works, but Jimmy was able to tell me that he was receiving signals that told him there had possibly been people living on Park Hall's site as early as Roman times. This is possible – a Roman road had been found many years earlier running parallel to the A49, and no doubt the land which now surrounds parts of the A49 in this area would have belonged to Park Hall centuries ago. It was at this part of the session that I was met by an enquiring look from Mark Leader, Park Hall's Managing Director. Fortunately Mr Leader is a very accommodating sort and happy in the knowledge that it was all for 'History', he carried on to his lunch.

As we were about to leave Park Hall, Jimmy mentioned that he could also detect ghosts with the help of his rod and, stopping at the front of the lake, he got out of the car and dowsed the lake. He said there was a spirit in the lake and that there were also five others in residence at Park Hall, but in different locations. He also believed that they had died at different periods of time.

I asked him to look at some of the stone in the buildings, to see how old it was and if any of it dated from pre-Norman times. He found this difficult, saying that some of the stone was very old and had been cut in different places. I have since found this to be true! John Rigby was developing Park Hall to such an extent that he had to bring in a lot of stone from other places and some of this got mixed in with stone already on the site. This explained what Jimmy Longton had told me.

After John had opened the Banqueting Hall, it wasn't long before he was ready to open the Hotel, Restaurant and the Cabaret Lounge. August 14th was the date set for the big night. Also to open about the same time was the Toby Snug Bar. Because of all the outside interest in Park Hall's redevelopment, the snug bar became an incredibly popular meeting place and continued to be so for many years. John Rigby's team of builders had worked from dawn until well into the night at times. The cabaret lounge had been built where the old function rooms had stood and from the demolition of the old building to the complete rebuild, it had taken only nine weeks.

Park Hall Cabaret Lounge was an amazing palace of entertainment and very plush, with 900 seats, where you could enjoy a meal as well as watching some of the best cabaret acts from around the world. It was full waitress service and no one was allowed to go to the bar but the waitresses. The first act to appear there was Peter Gordeno and his dancers and they opened fittingly, on John Rigby's birthday.

In 1973 Park Hall opened a 25-metre open-air swimming pool and the boating lake. The grounds were at this time being extensively landscaped. This included the valley where Camelot theme park is now situated, although John Rigby had other ideas for this site. As already mentioned, this valley was marked on earlier maps as 'Kiln Wood' and it is believed that the monks had kilns for firing their pottery situated there.

John's vision for this site was to construct an international showjumping arena.

By the end of 1973 John Rigby's ambition for Park Hall was no less than the first day he bought it. In fact, he was hell bent on expanding and improving what was already there. He decide to convert the outdoor pool into an indoor pool and by the side of the pool he planned to build tennis courts, a crazy golf course, children's playground and a 10-court squash club with two viewing courts that could seat up to one hundred spectators on each court – and he wanted all this ready for opening in the spring of 1974.

It was in February 1974 that I became involved with Park Hall. I had been invited to go for an interview for an assistant manager's job. My friend and future boss Dennis Houghton had arranged to have me picked up by the staff minibus driver, Dick Cox. Dick was a stone mason by trade and had worked for John on the building of the cabaret lounge. As we drove up the driveway past the side of the Cabaret Lounge, Dick pointed out to me a stone high up in the wall. It was an old round 'grind stone', the sort you would sharpen tools on. Dick told me it had been found buried in silt in the bottom of the lake when it had been drained. Dick had decided to make it a feature in the wall and had placed an old penny inside it when he laid it. He said it must have been very old and that it deserved a place in Park Hall's future. Dick was a wonderful old guy and took great pride in his work.

When I first set eyes on the swimming pool, it was a sorry sight. All that could be seen that February morning was mud and machines. What there was to see of the pool was a black muddy hole in the ground. John Rigby's plan to have it all up and running by Easter was beginning to look like a joke. I

Round stone set in the wall of the Cabaret Lounge by stonemason Dick Cox. It was found in the lake in 1972 when it was drained. Because of its age, Dick thought it should have its place in Park Hall's future and built it into the wall. After laying the stone, Dick placed an old penny inside it for luck. Photograph by Alec Price.

got the job and on Good Friday we opened against all the odds. Some of the paint was still wet and the tilers were still laying tiles on one of the pool sides. Dennis Houghton, the swimming pool manager, had worked right through the night and hadn't been home for twenty-four hours. He was shattered but his excitement at having made our deadline carried him through. After we closed that night we went for a well-earned drink, paid for by John Rigby.

With most of the Park Hall side of the complex now open, John could turn his attentions to Kiln Wood, or Arena North as it was to become known. With all the trees bulldozed and the sides of the valley shaped, it resembled a huge muddy pit, 1000 yards long and half as wide. John was busy planning his first event. This was to be the Dunhill International Horse Show and would take place on 30th June. As Arena North progressed, it began to look like a Roman ampitheatre. With open-plan seating on both hillsides, it resembled the coliseum; all that was needed were the gladiators!

View of the square. Photograph by Alec Price.

Arena North in 1978, an It's a Knockout show. Unfortunately a poor quality photograph but it does show the huge crowds that flocked to such events. Photograph by Alec Price.

This photograph shows only two walls of the original Hall still standing and knocked right back to the stonework. It was taken in 1972 when John Rigby was redeveloping the site. Many of the windows and doorways can be seen and matched to the photograph of the Hall taken in 1903. Sadly much of the interior woodwork and inner walls were in such a poor state that John Rigby had no choice but to almost completely rebuild the Hall.

6

The Showbiz Years

John decided he wanted someone of the highest calibre to run his operation at Arena North.

He recruited a man called Captain Christopher Coldrey. Capt Coldrey had recently been the national course builder for the South African Equestrian team. He was very highly regarded amongst the British showjumping fraternity and had often commentated on television for shows such as the Horse of the Year Show.

Capt Coldrey had a lot of influence and John knew he would have to use it to the best of his ability in order to attract the top stars for the Dunhill International Horse Show. Chris Coldrey pulled out all the stops and soon had names such as Harvey Smith, David Broome and Ted Edgar on the list for the show. The week before the show thousands and thousands of yards of turf arrived by the wagonload and men worked from dawn till dark laying it all. It was a race against time, but a race that John Rigby was determined he would win. Two days before the show was due to start I saw him drive down onto Arena North in his gold Rolls Royce, grab a bag of tools from the boot and in his expensive suit he went to work helping the joiners to put the finishing touches to the steps on the judges' tower.

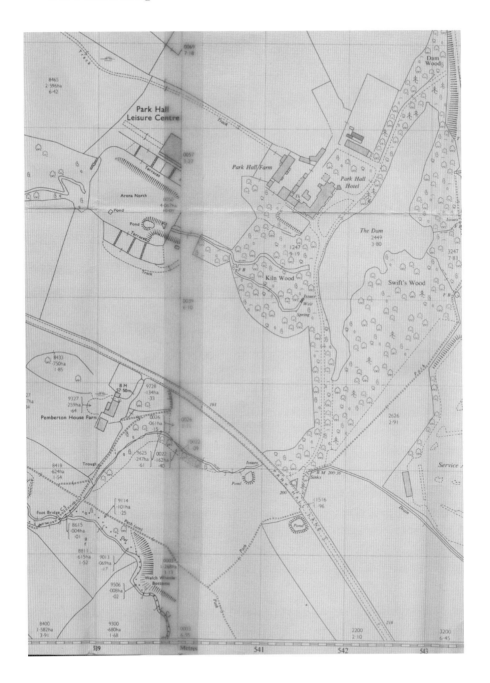

On 30th June it was all worthwhile: the show opened and Arena North was awash with colour and pageantry. Harvey Smith, David Broome and Ted Edgar, along with many other very famous names, competed. The show was a tremendous success. John Rigby had brought the biggest horse show ever to the North West. Indeed it was to be only the first of many and it was to be the first of many firsts. Arena North went on to host the July Wakes Festival for a number of years. This was a wonderful festival of music held in the Arena every summer and Park Hall hired the stage that the Rolling Stones had used for their concert in Hyde Park.

Over the four days that the Wakes Festival was running, an estimated 1,000 people camped in Park Hall's grounds – tents and caravans were squeezed into every field. The swimming pool was open twenty-four hours a day so that people could use the showers and toilets. The management at Park Hall allowed skinny-dipping in the pool between midnight and 6 a.m.! Security was high to make sure no one misbehaved, and to be fair no one did. Because of the musical content of the festival, the crowd's average agegroup was mid-twenties upwards, and apart from the odd person who had drunk too much, there was nothing that gave too much cause for concern.

Appearing were such stars as Barbara Dickson, Gallagher and Lyle and The Chieftains. One artist I will always remember was a singer who hosted the Saturday night show in 1977. His name was Noel Murphy. He was a big Irishman who was always drunk, but always a gentleman. Noel introduced me to Barbara Dickson and I've been a fan ever since. During the week Noel had been top of the bill in the Cabaret Lounge and although he was unheard of, the audiences loved him. Unfortunately, I have never seen or heard of him since!

Without doubt the biggest and most memorable event ever to take place at Park Hall was also in 1977, when MGM took over Arena North to film scenes for their film *International Velvet*. This was a sequel to the film *National Velvet*. They commandeered the whole site including the swimming pool laundry! Starring in the film and staying on site were some of the top film stars of the 1970s. Nanette Newman was one of the main characters of the film and staying there with her was her little girl, Emma Forbes. Miss Newman's husband, Bryan Forbes was the director. Also staying in the hotel was fifteen-year-old Tatum O'Neil, who played the lead role.

Filming for the scenes was only supposed to take ten days, but the weather was so poor that the crew ended up on site for three weeks. Due to the bad weather, most of the film crew spent their days in the Toby Snug Bar and by the time they had finished filming, they were true regulars. Members of the public were invited along as extras in the film and were paid £5 a day to take part in crowd scenes. Some people were paid more for certain scenes if they did some 'walk-on' parts, as they called them. Many of the actors used the swimming pool and other facilities on site during the time they were there. Arena North was also host to 'It's a Knockout' for the first time in 1977, which went on to be another of Park Hall's success stories.

All throughout the 1970s Park Hall was renowned for its

showbiz connections, the International Cabaret Lounge providing the venue for some of the acts of the era. The list of who appeared there could go on for ever. However I particularly remember the first time that Cannon and Ball appeared. It was in 1974 and they were a support act for Johnny Rae, who was trying to make a comeback. Johnny Rae had been a big star in the late 1950s to early 1960s. Sadly his comeback was short-lived. His act went down so badly that the management sacked him after only two nights and put Cannon and Ball to the top of the bill. They took the place by storm and were called back time and again for many years.

In that same year Park Hall brought Sacha Distel over from France. He was the biggest star to have appeared there up until then. It was for one night only and tickets were £5. It was a huge success, a complete sell-out. Many top acts soon followed, such as Tommy Cooper, Cliff Richard, (now Sir Cliff), Neil Sedaka, Russ Abbot and his band the Black Abbots and Bruce Forsyth, plus many more. The Toby Snug Bar that I mentioned earlier was used by many of the stars who stayed in the hotel and they could often be seen enjoying a drink with the locals before going on stage.

John Rigby sold Park Hall soon after he had got Arena North up and running. The brewers Bass North West became the new owners around the end of 1974. Capt Chris Coldrey took over as Managing Director with Bass, and in fairness it was Chris Coldrey who was responsible for many of Park Hall's successes during the mid- to late 1970s. It was certainly his prowess that contributed to the success of Arena North's showjumping spectaculars. In showjumping circles Park Hall/ Arena North was becoming as popular as Hickstead and

The Village Inn. This watering hole took over from the very popular Toby Snug Bar. Photograph by Alec Price.

Olympia. Many of the showjumping set actually preferred Arena North for its beautiful countryside and sumptuous facilities as well as its accessibility. Very few showjumping venues were as close to major motorway networks as Arena North was – literally right next to it. Many motorists used the Charnock Richard Service station on the M6 as a link to and from the motorway and although this was frowned upon by both the police and the motorway services, it was allowed to happen.

Having this access point was great for Park Hall. John Rigby and many of Park Hall's subsequent bosses have tried in vain to convince Lancashire County Councils Highways Department to install an access road. In 2004 the access from the motorway was shut off completely to all but service area staff and emergency services. The nearest access points to the M6 motorway are now approximately five miles in either direction.

In 1977 Park Hall's management looked at ways to cut costs, just as all companies do. They decided that they would experiment with the idea of covering the swimming pool over with a false floor during the winter months and using it as an exhibition hall. This they did and it proved so popular that it remained like that – they never re-opened it! They also gave up using the lake for boating and some other facilities were also axed in order to cut costs. The sad thing was that these were the facilities that used to attract families. Now, apart from the shows that Arena North staged during the summer months, there was very little to attract them. The cabaret was still ongoing, although this was also slowing down in the popularity stakes. By the early 1980s Bass North West wanted out.

In January 1980 John Rigby was back at the helm. His partner in this second ownership was Trevor Hemmings, who now also owned Pontins Holiday centres. But by 1982 John was sole owner. John Rigby could see that Park Hall needed something that would bring back the families. All the original ideas had gone and new things had to be developed. In 1982 John decided to completely redevelop the valley where Arena North had served so well for the past eight years. His idea was to create a medieval theme park. His initial idea was for moving monsters, dragons and an adventure land. He decided to call it Camelot. As this project began to take shape, ideas grew and rides were soon to become a feature, as was the introduction of the jousting arena – King Arthur and his knights arrived.

During his quest for the history of Park Hall John Rigby had spoken to a professor from Manchester, who studied the legend of King Arthur. The professor told John that he believed King Arthur may well have spent time in this area that we now call Park Hall. His theory was that the legendary king had visited a monastery that was on Park Hall land – long before St Cuthbert's time. The reason for his visit was to try to raise an army and Park Hall was a safe meeting place.

As well as his plans for Camelot, John Rigby also had massive plans for the Park Hall side of the site. He extended the Hotel, built extensive Conference and Banqueting facilities and sold off some land to various companies including Bloemandhaal Garden Centre. In 1985 Park Hall changed its name to Park Hall Leisure plc and was floated on the OTC market. In that same year John also built and opened the Spanish Village, along with a new health club and swimming pool. In March 1986 the company was sold to Granada Leisure plc. John Rigby stayed on for a time, working with Granada as a consultant and manager. He finally bowed out for the last time in March 1988.

This is what he told me when I spoke to him in 2003:

> *'I absolutely love the place and would love another crack at running Park Hall. I believe I have one last big project left in me and I would like that to be Park Hall ... Who knows?'*

After John left, Park Hall and Camelot both continued to grow. Over the next ten years Park Hall extended its Hotel as well as its Conference and Banqueting facilities. By this time the Cabaret Lounge had ceased to be and was now a Nightclub and Disco, re-named the 'Park Nightstyle'. The squash club had been sold, as had the exhibition halls. The Toby Snug Bar had been closed down, relocated, and renamed 'The Village Pub'. Camelot was also doing very well and was voted the North West's top tourist attraction, welcoming more and more visitors every year.

However by 1998 all was not well, for although things were heading in the right direction, Granada Leisure plc were getting itchy feet and were talking of selling. Bosses at Park Hall decided that this was a huge opportunity for them and a management buyout was discussed. Granada's reasons for wanting to sell were said to be 'directional'. They wanted to move away from the theme park activities to concentrate on other things. The proposed buyout by the management went ahead and the new company was formed. Park Hall's new owners became 'Prime Resorts'. It was to be business as usual with more improvements planned in every direction.

Under Prime Resorts, Park Hall and Camelot were looking good. King Arthur was still very much in residence. Not only did he officiate at Camelot, he was often found holding court in the Banqueting Hall where he hosts many a medieval feast. Camelot again won the Top Tourist award, this time under Prime Resort's leadership.

It was also around this time that Park Hall took the decision to close down its nightclub and for some years it remained closed and soon became unusable as a facility. Its only function was that of a storeroom. This must have been a headache for the management, to have such a fine building standing empty and deteriorating. It was even considered converting it in to more hotel bedrooms or conference suites. The room was by now in such a state of disrepair that no matter what it was to be used for, it was going to need a huge investment. Prime Resorts made up their mind to re-open it as a nightclub. Once the decision had been taken, it was full steam ahead and no expense was spared. 'The Park Nightclub' was going to be the best around. The cost: £1m. It re-opened in the summer of 2002.

The author in front of the old part of the hotel. Photograph by Dr David Sands.

7

Park Hall's Ghosts

Park Hall is no different to any other establishment that is centuries old in that there are ghostly tales to be told. This is the one chapter of this book that I have really wanted to write. When I decided to write Park Hall's history I already knew of its spooky past – or at least some of it! As well as asking members of Park Hall's staff I wrote to the *Chorley Guardian* asking them to put an appeal in the paper for anyone who had a story to tell to get in touch with me. The response I got was limited but nevertheless good.

It was also another area in which I used the talents of Jimmy Longton 'the dowser'. I knew that Jimmy had appeared on TV with Jane Goldman and in the programme Jim had shown off his prowess at getting rid of spirits from a house. Not that I wanted Jim to remove any spirits from Park Hall! I just wanted to know if he believed any actually existed on Park Hall's site. Jims answer to my question was that he believed six ghosts were in residence at Park Hall. He told me that they had all died at different periods of time and that they were to be found in various parts of the site. One was in the lake, three were in the Hall itself and two were wanderers. He said he had a strong feeling of a presence around the Dungeon

Bar in the Banqueting Hall. John Rigby had told me of a cleaner who had gone into the Dungeon Bar one day and fled, screaming that someone was hanging in there. Further inspection found nothing, but the woman described the victim as an old man with a beard and dressed in old robes.

I mentioned earlier in the book that this was the area where the foundations had been discovered, believed to have dated back to pre-Norman times, which could quite easily have been the foundations of the monastery. Jim had also mapped this out to be what he described as either a chapel or a church.

Eerie photograph of the inside of the Dungeon Bar. This area is said to be one of the spookiest places on site. People have spoken of 'having a feeling of being watched' in here. It was from here that a cleaner ran out screaming that she had seen a man hanging. However, further investigation revealed nothing. Photograph © Park Hall.

It was in the Banqueting Hall that a strange occurrence happened when I was working at Park Hall during the 1970s. I think it was 1977 or 1978. Park Hall's housekeeper and two of her staff had been in the Banqueting Hall setting up for a wedding one Friday afternoon. The wedding reception was to be held in the Banqueting Hall the following day. After they had finished setting everything out, including putting the cake on the table, the housekeeper locked up the Hall and went home for the day, taking the keys with her, knowing full well that she would be back to work first thing in the morning. The lady in question had worked at Park Hall since John Rigby had opened in 1972 and was most trustworthy. The following morning when she unlocked the Banqueting Hall, she could not believe her eyes. Everything she and her two colleagues had set out the afternoon before had been removed and the Hall had been set up for a medieval feast. The cake, glasses and all the cutlery had been placed carefully on the stage in the hall. Nothing was broken or damaged. The Hall was in a locked state when the housekeeper arrived, and from her leaving the previous evening to her arriving on the Saturday morning absolutely no one had had access to the Hall.

One phone call I received following the *Chorley Guardian* article was from a lady who had worked at Park Hall during the 1970s. This lady did not want to give her name because she said she felt 'a bit of a fool'. This is her story.

'I arrived for work as usual, about 7.30 in the morning. I went through Hotel reception – this was the old reception near the porch at the front of the building – I said 'Good Morning' to the hotel receptionist and then I went through the restaurant, up the stairs and towards the Cabaret Lounge. You had to walk along a corridor and to the right was the stage, to the left and up a few stairs were

the dressing rooms. I had gone into the Cabaret Lounge to fetch something and was returning to Hotel reception. As I was walking past the stairs to the dressing room, I noticed someone out of the corner of my eye, stood at the top of the stairs, I just said 'Good Morning' and carried on. When I got back to reception I remarked that it was early for them to be starting rehearsals. I was asked what I meant. I told them that I had just seen someone in fancy dress, like a monk, by the dressing rooms.

At which I was told there was no one in there and there was certainly no rehearsals going on at 7.30 in the morning. The receptionist said, 'You've just seen a ghost!' It didn't frighten me and I laughed it off at the time, but it has made me wonder over the years.'

When I told Mark Leader what this lady had told me, he said the passageway I had spoken of was always freezing cold.

John Rigby told me of another incident that happened in a part of the Hall not far from this. It happened at the time he was doing all the redevelopment, in 1972. John had a huge team of builders and joiners working from dawn until well into the night. This particular night, as on other nights, all the crew stopped work at about 7 p.m. for a break. They would all congregate downstairs for a cup of tea and a chat. One night one of the joiners didn't come down. Someone went to look for him but couldn't find him anywhere; his jacket and his tools were where he was supposed to be but no sign of him! The following day he arrived on site and asked if someone would collect his things – he said he did not want to go inside himself to get them. John Rigby told one of the men to find out why he was so upset and why he didn't want to work there any more. Eventually the site manager had a word with him and was told the night before the joiner had been working outside Room 10. He walked inside to get something and as he did he saw something walk towards him.

The entrance to the Dungeon Bar. Photograph by Alec Price.

It went straight through him, and the door slammed shut! He said he could not get the door open again. Panicking, he eventually climbed out of a window and ran.

John Rigby and some of the other men tried to recreate the same scenario but no-matter how they tried, they could not make it happen!

Park Hall's most documented ghost is 'The Lady of the Lake', sometimes referred to as 'The Grey Lady' or even more recently 'The Blue Lady'. Legend has it that during

Elizabethan times the Hoghtons gave shelter to priests and monks who were threatened with persecution. It was while one of these priests was in residence at Park Hall, that a young local maiden fell in love with the priest and became pregnant by him. However, when her condition came to light, she was shunned and told never to come to Park Hall again. The poor young woman was so distraught that she decided to take her life. She threw herself into the lake and drowned.

Over the years people who have seen her describe the sighting as astonishing. She is said to rise out of the water, and her beauty and the glow that she radiates pales everything around her grey. During George Few's time, various local policemen on patrol, both on foot and on cycle are said to have seen this apparition and were stunned by the astonishing beauty of the girl. When I spoke to Mark Leader about the Park Hall ghosts, he told me of a member of staff who had seen the Lady of the Lake recently. He said that he had no reason to disbelieve this person and that because of her account of what she had seen he believed her. This lady now lives in Hertfordshire. Mark gave me her name and address and I have written to her twice to ask her what she saw that night, but sadly, she has not replied to either of my letters!

The story of the Lady of the Lake is mentioned in a number of books about Lancashire's ghosts and haunted houses. She is sometimes confused with the White Lady of Samlesbury Hall, near Blackburn. However, the two are not connected.

It would be easy to get carried away with ghost stories in a place such as this and with so many people available to comment on who saw what and how such-a-body saw something.

Park Hall's Lake. Well documented as being the home of the famous 'Lady of the Lake' ghost. When it was drained in 1972, objects were found that dated back to the days of the monastery. It was also from here that much of the stone used in the building of the original Hall was hewn. This wonderful lake has been used for fishing and boating in its time. It is now just a feature of beauty with its spectacular water fountain. Photograph by Dr David Sands.

I have just highlighted some of the stories that I consider to be the best. I would also like to add that I have not heard one story where any of the ghosts here at Park Hall have tried to harm anyone or cause any kind of mischief ... so sleep well!

The author in the reputedly haunted Dungeon Bar. Photograph by Dr David Sands.

8

The Future

Wouldn't it be wonderful if we could soar through time like 'Superman' flying high above Park Hall, taking in all the events that have happened here? We could watch George Few to see if he really did get up to some of the things he is reputed to have done. We could witness the Civil War and the Catholic persecutions in Elizabethan times. The Jacobean uprising, the family feuds and the gluttony, the Banastre Rebellion and the Battle of Preston. For me the most interesting time to see would be the pre-Norman years, the time when the monks were here and more especially the three years that St Cuthbert's body was said to have been laid at rest here, hidden in the woods, woods that today's members of the public enjoy at their leisure.

So very much has happened since 886AD and so many changes have taken place, which is not surprising. The management at Park Hall are committed to the future. Plans for sustained growth aimed at the leisure facilities are constantly being discussed and more investment means more employment. With a company the size of Park Hall, changes of direction are inevitable and can there be any greater change of direction than from the monastery of a Saint, to a valley full of rollercoaster rides overseen by a king?

Mark Leader, Park Hall's Operations Director. Photograph © Park Hall.

(Top) Mark Leader with the author outside the new hotel entrance. (Bottom) Front view of the old porch entrance to the hotel. Both photographs by Dr David Sands.

Front view of the Hotel entrance. Photograph by Alec Price.